Refuge(e)

David Paul Mesler

The author's inspirations include: The interior life; the maturing of the spiritual and psychological self; the complexity of human community; the search for inspiration and love; Theodore Roethke's idea that every line is its own poem; creating sparks by juxtaposing words; working from grids of favorite words; the deepening of meaning through repetition; dream states; ordering poems into a chronology; fractured narratives with flipping perspectives; the simplicity and immediacy of the couplet; the various impacts of the short line; and the flow experience produced by space on the page.

To be read aloud.

when solitary
I perceive only agony

the sounds of void
the skip of psyche

I advise my lunatic
to quote something solid

to magnify the circumference
to check what's here

but I was marked
as a child

with an eventual
epilogue

barriers
of mammoth proportions

a final swim
to source

to sense the spheres
behind the tears

how many unsettled
days and years

go into the preview
of heaven sent

the community of angels
quiet and bent

waiting at the bedside
of renters who

no longer can afford
to live

he, surprisingly
was a melody

a song about gardens
in winter

about the deep play
of warm reds weaving

the harvest that was thick
and full of praise

but also about
the fight over cliffs

the rocks
that were thrown

the wave that covered him
and others

how a dream is left
in his place

thin legs
and running

bath water
children

happily naked
in snow

distant soldiers
picking up arms

*

my overwhelming self
comic and proud

victorious
over no one

*now planting willows
in the dark*

*I guess I've supposed
and opposed enough*

*strategized encounters
to death*

*sullen around
perceived neglect*

*pretending to be well
at the well's bottom*

*support comes
in a pocket of nowhere*

*sweet meager sunlight
on an absolute leaf*

*the star that plays
on a bit of water*

*the shoe you dropped
when you ran*

4

when bridges carelessly made
collapse

break in the rocks
and water below

oh the benefit
of mature quests

the greeting
of another ecstatic

do you remember hope
I do

let's do hope
together

a surprising trail
mysteriously opens

crowded by trees
molting moss

tribes of wildlife
skitter and swoop

rattle bushes
scale trunks

a lone howl holds
its purest note

no, it isn't me
no, it isn't you

graveyards of toes
talons, knees

the roots of centuries
buckle

we wade into seas
of giant ferns

the brightening shafts of searchlight
filter

watch your face
your eyes, your breathing

dust likes to dance
with little wings in flight

vivid are the green frogs
bulging, singing

proudly
of rougy marrow

mosquitoes enlarge
with blood on your arm

the essence of night
starts to purple

toward the cliff
and the water we go

where starshine lives
and the moon rules

follow where the heavy
but light heart leads

to where flashes liven
the landscape

where the edges of clarity
are clear

so crisp
you can draw them on paper

on the new beach
morning comes like love

a dawn of strange
but familiar colors

forward is a boat
our size and shape

behind
a history of night

a cocoon day
and finally

interior sculpting
harmonizing with birds

pre-song
pre-words

naked and clean
inside spun spins

a bright boy dance
under the covers

an angel
telling itself stories

a riot of rain
on the panes

sheets of flash
and warning

mature girls
already out for a walk

twirling umbrellas
stopping for cats

but you
a cocoon

and finally
snug

making wings
blinding and beatific

surrounded by layers
of sheer over sheer

you may as well sleep
and dream

maybe the birth
of smile-crying cheeks

no roads
no rules

*just open, endless
creaks*

*for now, though
a sliver of sheen*

*nested
in*

*waiting without waiting
for the moment that's yours*

*the riot of need
to be free*

*immense portrait
staying true to pursuits*

*sturdy amid danger
cultivated at the feast*

*rejoicing
at remaining nameless*

*and alarmed
by no fear*

*flip the face
a fresh portal*

*helpless and heaving
desiring parasites*

*rearranged features
that are shapeless spoils*

*flashes of too little
too late*

*oh exterior's richness
and history*

*a brave benevolence
for the ages*

*oh interior's
inferiority*

*the harsh and daily
hari-kari*

*

*I've buried
all that was real to me*

my dreams
along with frustrations

what I'd protected
for so long

the things
I laughed about

how I starved for days
curtains I drew

where I took refuge
when paralyzed

the curl of my hair
the squalor of my sheets

the pages
that tallied up the costs

pastries and fervor
stop signs and hearths

all far below
any cellar

deep in the dirt
where nothing dwells

deep in a heart
long gone

beyond the worms
insects, roots

beyond stream
and steam

in the core so thick
and thorough

it hardly can be called
earth

I suspect the real
is still real and there

just not to me
or anyone else

a dance compressed
tantalizing, obscure

with no music
or reason, or room

I go along
with my basic business

placate here
turn west there

a zealot
who's lost their fever

a singer
without a song

a lecture hall
filled with dicks and diction

liquor bottles
with hundreds of handprints

minds cut
and sewn back together

chisels working
at fossils of dishes

red petals fall
from the blue blue sky

a beloved swoons
gracefully

a platter of varicose veins
sits

ribbons
cut to ribbons

like all tales
this tale's one of longing

pulsating proud
for an eye and a lick

hoping to find
the light in blight

praying for trees
and getting a stick

*

cathedrals of energy
ease and eddy

into the design
of his restless difficult

an alchemy sweet
from rogue to tender

to life
in the scenic miracle

paper is paper
after all

sin
can be forgiven

whatever is past
is long past now

when counted
by the nanos of creation

feeling free
to feeling speak

to the great
amused choreographer

must you delight
in my klutzy temple

the faceplant and fury
of my saddened joke

must you make a ministry
of every little thing

*turn my three-leaf clover
into four*

*but the anger
is replaced*

*by a spell of well
and oh well*

*he looks at hard blessings
anew*

*every wrinkle
a well-earned gash*

*slimmed to a brief
remembrance*

*

*freshly charged
I cycle through graces*

*spill fresh ink
duplicate swans*

*create a sanctuary
of berries and stories*

aqua possibilities
kinship with weeds

volumes of script
and stepping stones

voices from the sky
music from bones

a wild mixing
of scrupulous thought

dionysian dance
jackrabbit dreams

I capture
what I can

until heavier looks
upon heavier books

bury
my eyes

until quicksand
swallows my hat

and my waving fingers
succumb

*you may walk over
the deserted maroon*

*the pulse precise
long gone*

*pick up the charge
unknowingly*

*pick up your pace
decide to write*

*cover how you covered
your late rejoice*

*until colors couldn't help
but show through*

*carry your east
to the west of west*

*and pass your papers
to the next*

*tomorrow is nervous
giddy for you*

it strolls in riddles
and rapture

hopes to write your name
in blood

on the deep curl
of amen

it prays you arrive
in shade and schism

a midnight crack
of lightning dawn

so it can invent
a long road jumping

with wet
white pearls

then a noon
so commanding

that all clocks
stop

but go when the big boat
of night approaches

*such wriggling minutes
bottles to be smashed*

*bubbles in champagne
await contained*

*oh mighty tomorrow
holds its trumpet up*

*the games
about to begin*

*a ferment just for you
whirls turbulent*

*behind
the sudden gate*

*I'm brilliantly chained
I pulsate blind*

*my deafness
can be bliss*

*I'm ministered by the astral
have evidence of blink*

of the universe coming
and going

stars kissing
when they drink

who's the hero
in this story

power is
as power does

all beyond
our little loops

and what we think
we think

I'm brilliantly chained
I pulsate blind

every visual
visualized

every moment
in the moment

lived
and brightly realized

*

she's eclipsed
back to the breath

he's remote
back to the breath

belongings are seized
keys swiped

rotten boards
break through

but you are back
to the breath

back to cherishing
every inhale

every slow
fullsome fall

back to radiant
design and delight

understanding
every rise and release

that nothing needs
to be understood

rugged muscles
are severed from the bone

final words
are mumbled

everyone chewing
bad habits

they've been working on
since infancy

but you
are back to the breath

back away
from any tendency

to chisel and chunk
or hammer and blow

or spin
or silently explode

because
all else can collapse

she can faint
he can freeze

grumble and curse
or worse

furniture thrown
fire started

lights snap out
walls shift

windows buckle
and smash

testamentary papers
falling as ash

but you
remain a spark

a
joy

breathing
only breathing

breathing
only breathing

*there and watchful
but also not*

*no, so very much
not*

*sustainable sadness
has shut me down*

*dissolved
the only world I've known*

*they counsel carousels
over me*

*choose rats and crows
instead*

*I stare
at others' encounters*

*choke at any brief mention
of youth*

*accuse whoever
of intimate error*

undress to die
in drafts

whatever dreams I had
are left hungry

grow
to monstrous vacuums

whatever wishes I had
are spoiled

infinitely heavy
with regret

ripe lips call out
numerous names

none of them mine
though I wait

and carefully expose
my reliable nature

how my yearning to possess
has ceased

*

my melancholy
is stately

I'm handling the drought
quite well

shock transmuted
to sincerity

wriggle and ripple
to silent feign

be assured, though
climate lives

here
and how

and it's anything
but subtle

fuck how it happened
whoever was involved

fuck the whole lot
fuck you all

*

sometimes rough
can help the healing

frantic can tend to
and correct the depth

you may rehearse drowsy
or trumpet away busy

feel safe either way
in your belonging, then crack

totality startles
peril comes close

change
gets awfully curious

smelling
the very go of you

lemon sweat
hints of greed

skin that hitches
on nails

but in you go
to the mess of vines

safe until snakes
with minds of their own

possessed with getting
at the truth

hungry for false flesh
they peel away

shall we ascend
to the entrance

the final embrace
of forever

or shovel down
and chronicle dirt

the layers
we encounter

pursue a cure
improvise steadfast

repeat the answers
of salvation

or weigh ourselves down
with iron chains

challenge the deep bones
of stuck

return to the center
that's larger than the whole

or wrap the little spider's web
around us

grow in holiness
and greet the angels

or smack ourselves
till we're strewn

disciplined
or random

clarity
or chaos

rapture
or rust

light
or fight

the tension is additional
withdrawal not an option

we cannot shy away
and sleep

of course
we know the answer

but oxygen
distracts

so do fingers
and squirrels

and papers
and planes

funny fallacies
and facts

many are frozen
by suppose

pros and cons
cons and prose

for the millionth time
snap and snap to

see the universe
for what it is

I nurse a laugh
back into the unknown

squint at their sour
hurricane

illuminate their biting
bitter torrential

shut down
before the end begins

quartets and quintets
play on the banks

openly scuttle
with unfunny humor

random tangents
associating wordles

clever edifices
popping girdles

*oh bilious bubbles
and saliva strands*

*your hateful takedowns
of serious stands*

*deliriously you borrow
jerry-rigged jokes*

*through stomach and back
you poke your pokes*

*bloodless statuary
of history may fall*

*but rocks of now
may uppercut your call*

*I need to just stare
at the carpet*

*watch my fist
for hours*

*do nothing, be nothing
unagreeably*

*see if my knuckle-skin
grows*

*give me a moment
a hundred years or so*

*I'll be back, I imagine
to crawl*

*to kid
the toying tyranny again*

*resume
my resident muddle*

*you say you miss
the me of yore*

*wild mimic
of face and song*

*the loony
of my magic tricks*

*occasional shitpan
of wit*

*I never want
to disappoint*

but I may be a while
an echoing while

standing parallel
in the doorway

unable to shift
or shuffle

needing the silence
and deep freeze

to be unknown
in my shackled shock

poor alone me
I cannot float

what work was I doing
what day is it

sensual furniture
hastens around

glassware seeks
the dishes

earth spins faster
than I can notice

*the strobing of the sun
speeds beyond flicker*

*the rise and after
soon long gone*

*

*apparently
on this smudgy date*

*of ash and hang
and blindfolded bottles*

*I'm to christen
the fair backwards*

*resurrect
past obsessions*

*go forward
without the poverty of law*

*nourish myself
on the fun best*

*on cream and laughter
kindness and quiet*

let parts of old skeletons
dig and die

let old skins harden
in the sun

how far I've fallen
it doesn't matter

ground zero
is wherever I'm at

regression
isn't an option

I'm propelled, alive
and there's no going lower

there's no crucifying
a volcano

*

the come-to-light sham
is bearable

if unwritten shadows
retreat

the lonely chamber
hospitable

if conflict and girth
are hollowed out

remove the lewd
leave the bare walls

pray for warmth
from the chill

remove the iris
leave the pupil

know the mountain
in the hill

we advance
so slowly

but we do
advance

retain the one or two
true gradual valuables

slough off the piles
of needless clothes

toss aside the random
bric-a-brac

outside we collide
with other whites of eyes

supposed lovers
withhold

others multiply
like ones and zeros

in computer generated
games

motionless though
we transfuse confusion

make something singular
from plethora to pure

a grain of good
a drop of rain

a word of friendship
a buried atom

finally the antidote
to smothering sickness

*the open, barless
prison*

*think about that
what does it mean to you*

*got any ideas
can you see anything*

*does that surprise you
make you feel comfortable*

*do you shut down
and turn the page*

*do you slam doors
louder than necessary*

*a wild man napping
can you see that*

*him crouched and eating
think about it*

*the numbers he draws
with feathers and thorns*

the maps he makes
with draperies

how he brushes the earth
with his bare feet

flees in and out
of your memory

does that surprise you
him fleeing

are you comfortable
when he returns

the stark sinew
as he thinks

about
a woman

the dusk darkening
his hooded eyes

do you shut down
and turn the page

do you leave
slamming the door

what do you make
of an empty window casing

of the grand dawn
rising like life itself

and the man drinking
from a pottered cup

then smashing it
and looking at you

would you rather
he hand you a priceless jewel

what would that mean
to you

would you rather he run
lean and gazelle-like

over plains
that take hours to cross

and you watching
until he's an ant

finally pinched
into the horizon

*

*what's buried
whispers*

*the kingdom
rolls*

*lungs flourish
spells shower*

*a theatrical swoop
from the attic*

*along with a mass
of rattles*

*sicklysweets
have soaked too long*

*kicks don't like
their tiny rectangle*

*a bounty of hurt
drives up from the center*

*matchless laughter
lets itself out*

*hallelujah
and horrible harangue*

*the there with hair
arises*

*no one recognizes
the arriving gob*

*not even you
and it's yours*

*who would've known
years ago*

*that I'd become
a mute*

*gash at my weight
shatter drinks*

*run away
from fresh honey*

*but names
were named*

fakes
became breakable

the deaf
were allowed to hear

every tender touch
was observed up close

the supple
were allowed to breathe

too thirsty
I was

too
intimately hungry

stumbling
in clumsy afterlifes

too happy
I was

too fogged up
fogged in

believing
in love's generosity

*a statue
made of flesh*

*that can cry
on cue*

*I waited in a state
of unsuffering shock*

*pillows languorous
sleeping in sweetness*

*clouds brushing
a silent sky*

*then what
was in store*

*strengthened
darkened*

*swept in
and suggested I leave*

*

*pop the cork
champagne for all*

blossoms
in our prime

tales told
with wild coincidence

and diction to strike
and savor

can you still taste
the dank fever

of past
acrobatics

synchronize with yesterday's
longing for crumbs

are you lively
to naive hundreds

that live abustle
inside of you

can you enunciate
post-liquor

pre-
and during, too

petals and tongues
stalks out walking

we lick and take
our licking

corners perplex
and promise adventure

until the blind man's
sticking

she clings to hallways
lowers stars

lays dreams out
on the table

mends
infinite crazy quilts

poised
in mouthless solitude

occasionally she faces
forever

suffers
a strange joy

hears an audience
cheer her on

cuts ties
with weeping

oh
randomized meditation

skipping from oval
to oval

magnetic scissors
find her

her fabric
and her thread

oh rooms
of shifting light

singing squares
of hallelujah

may she find deep reason
to pray

let in
the displacing wind

she's a mentor
to begin

to the infinite lake
of find

ties up the walls
of their cocoon

waits for her satchel
to exercise

to press
its lifelines out

oh the first half-asleep walk
of sleepwalk

the novelty
of fresh fascination

how they cross
the criss of humming

the rivers
of flowers and food

agree to not wail
or argue or stop

to play all the plays
unrude

thumb the thrumming
of hearts and heads

exhale
the scent of centuries

fiddle out
the five fingered masterpiece

peek at the boo
not you, yes you

peek at the boo
not you

pretend to be meager
about what's in store

then wow the floor
the door, the snore

*wow the new
of every you*

*the new
of every wowing new*

*shoes are visible sometimes
everything else, haze*

*tall is slick
whistling somewhere*

*up close is riot
hue and tendril*

*every tail whips
for front of line*

*every taunt
is astounding*

*but back up, boy
and it's a blur*

*waste of stew
and brown*

reach in to the end
of your sleeve, dear

pull out
what you can

children, old folks
teddy bears, kitchen wares

before the foul cloud
catches fire

a mythic ballet
in the womb

verses wait
to be expressed

warbles and shrieks
hidden in the slit

angle to be
the next witness

throw aside
the blankets and sheets

the sun is gliding
and gilding the room

bring the sloshing water
and spillage

swoon and dread
by the bed

observe the rounded
bulging servant

steady your shaking
shivering hands

the word of words
is being born

the O of oh
the I of eye

the new from growing old
is torn

her days are frantic
with little people

getting their names
right

taking care
to tie their tumbles

congregate sports
open their bows

shall we complete
our maybes today

capture mist
lure in the fish

cast our beams
on the middle of the night

consider
the star's wish

recall last week's
thunder shower

are you or you
scared of it now

she enlivens
each little squirmy person

*to curious
personhood*

*points to the ticking
slash of time*

*says goodbye
with a snapping song*

*they'd like
to know math*

*the way they do
the alphabet*

*at least
on this frozen afternoon*

*when fierce owls
who*

*and radical alleys
speed*

*and teacher heels elicit
direct confrontation*

they'd like to dine
on pop quizzes

so easy they add them
like butter to corn

so natural
they snap fingers and flare

figure the physics
of inverted air

by picturing elevators
flying through space

clocks that don't tick
that have lost their face

trains crisscrossing
their heres and theres

stars that don't know
their negative place

pencils tap
then are gripped by misers

who don't know how much
they have or had

numbskulls aflutter
grow numb with time

thinking about
the power of pop

when needles prick
ever tighter balloons

and that's their heads
buffled buffoons

they feel their half-life
spilling decay

don't care what comes
just please come what may

last problem, the rate
at which objects sink

when dropped stories high
into misery

mother splits
from her singing

the daffodil prayer
turns to clutter

how did sun and choir
turn to mess

ceremony of grow
gets frittered away

now she sits
with brown apparitions

a smattering
of pink debris

feeling stern
she wants others to ache

to unembrace
and walk away

no more caressing
only grasping what's left

no more conversation
just the last gasp

a window where you
can see lean bodies

gather to eat
around bouquets

I've been scoffed at
sure

been told
I'm a spectacle

too full of sugar
and fake sonnets

a scrape
that barely survived

that I'm a husband
too full of animals

a pet
that refuses to consume

a solo act shrinking
as it paints past contacts

a revolt
with nothing to push against

here
take my theatrical scarf

I'm amassing my luggage
and dreams

goodbye to the fold
where I landed awhile

no need to drink
a spot of pity for me

no need to see
the shoving off

there'll just be shrugs
and oh well

but I'll be leaning toward
a striking new dawn

waving to colors
pastel

be patient
daily, in the corner

this brief whole
is a blessing

toughen
the current moment

raise your face
to the filling shine

in the midst of beasts
and chaos

feeling so lean
without a name

temptations taken
drown in the shallows

withdraw to the top
of the island

divide your hesitations
until they're conquered

succulent swearing
renounce

lean toward your destiny
of float and formless

picking you up
the wind of innocence

*

thunder slips into ears
and out his saying mouth

lakes make their way
to his hands

he gazes at necks
gauges winds

a loaf of bread
scolds the table

summer seems
to have given him the slip

heaven decides
to lay on him

his father mixing
the day's drink

*

he thrives
on the mind's fury

every gesture
unfinished

proud of playful roses
gone black

conducting breezes
in vain

too busy
for real sorrow

always in attempt
at geometry far

hypnotized
by his own sprouts

that refuse to fit
their rooms

maybe broken triangles
are the answer

he goes full throttle
in a tangled direction

maybe it should be
satinsmooth

he dreams a texture
of sleep till sleep

waking enflamed
he jumps up and out

taking on multiple muses
with muscle

frolic and fight
off on a tangent

fume and forget
undone dozens

curious corners
of promising crumbs

calculations scribbled
and tossed

when graphing
his identity

he discovered
a watch in the clover

an undulating
midday

a flying carpet
on exhibit

a scared scribble
that sobbed

a growing sentiment
hanging with sludge

a link to another burst
of morning

feet puttering
past entrances

journals
full of breasts and chests

twigs that rooted
and grew to trees

grips that gripped
each other

a stage within stages
set for one

the universe
an unblinking eye

so this is how it feels
when surrender is solitary

and instinct
augments

when wrestling worries
gives way to voyage

and the prop-up by friends
with the same old stories

of tiny stalls
and fragrant honks

makes room
for ever-so-slight new juice

of newfound
flesh

*yes, I've had enough
of lived-in wrap*

*and warp that confuses
my senses*

*I'm ready to walk
the slimmering shallows*

*and approach the wave
that is mine*

*my endless instinct
for solace and rays*

*plus massive cluster
of prism days*

*make for a life
of wrangled fragment*

*and now I sit
in riches*

*kicks at bolder
stone and nail*

arms of lengthy
pratfall humor

eyes and tongue
of care and might

thoughtful nods
nodding off

wake up, wake up
the details shine

in reflective gloss
and gleam

groggy middle-nights
fended-off fights

live on
in many a mirror

once so sure
of hardened mountains

emotions questioned
for their texture

I'm ready to render
elegant

whatever and whomever
passes

why not commend
the overbake try

clap
for sensory overload

playfully string
bad marionettes

dance dumb and dumber
under the rope

all your yous
eventually build

a sturdy swirl
of the half-forgotten

salutary sugars
empathetic flights

the bounding regal
and the rotten

fast it goes
and here it is

the hiss
of unknown origin

random pictures
catching fire

the end
of all your beginnings

I'm tired
of tonguing riddles

revolving
in my own doors

taking shelter
in curtains

being disappointed
in my tears

the yoke of serious
declared itself early

welcomed weight
and deep dives

perfection and polish
were to hide behind

but haze
was lovelier and truer

I'm what happens
when you wash the fog

more of the impossible
fog plus steam

low low clouds
of long reflection

floating countries
of dream

I'd like to invoke
informal scenes

whims
without good reason

broad guffaws
from yammering maws

jokes that skim
and don't deepen

enough of intricate
evangelization

tantalizing others
with long trains of thought

I speak now only
when spoken to

think, too
in monosyllabic

a post traumatized brain
and drain

finally happy
with my sighs and shrugs

she's an inward creature
a tunnel of crows

thick with sinking
in labor with believe

a scrap that doesn't
know how to receive

*a stitch that's been
unravelled*

*the everlasting
is lost on her*

*being filled with solar
is a bad dream*

*she likes to juxtapose
pieces from puzzles*

*place her palms
over candles lit*

*her blend is dark
and sour and rotten*

*she eats what needs
to be thrown up and out*

*still it takes courage
to create bad drama*

*to play its central character
to the balconies*

*

I pray
trying not to scream

over the spiral
of catacombs

one by one
replace ugly caves

with humankind
and kindness

the sunny spread
of benediction

the weep of floodgates
holding firm

no use in recounting
terror's toll

I run toward tender
look and keep

I've had enough
of predatory challenge

I wish for the wash
of postlude

craggy voice ragged
from squelched yelling

being overtaken
by anticipation's clamp

the harm of my body's
search and seizure

invented hover over
supposed leisure

once again sit
in the face of the act

of sitting
just sitting

and noting
the break

the sun
and water

finding its way
from out of the clouds

out of the clouds
out of the clouds

for a brilliant time
of its choosing

*

I need a mansion
of oxygen

a host
made of unlit space

a stage where heels
click and clack

and lyrics
vicariously rise

I guess I'm ridiculous
theater

making choices
of survive and respect

that writes new manuscripts
of elusive scene

about most and more
and eventually less

master
of the acoustical shell

the proscenium arch
the set and design

boards hold up
the walls and stairs

doors and windows
go nowhere

I flame as an only
in the spotlight

on the outskirts
of the skirt

make a speech
about droning-on dignity

without any dignity
at all

naked and shaking
shaking-cold

counting the scores
for and against

ask about putting
an end to the ending

letting the card house
fall

letting the old man
loosen and collapse

back
to an unbreathing ball

*

left lonely
by the sermon

he's a voice
without freedom

a cheek
with no intimacy

a motive
without a task

so
he shrivels

but then
he refuses to shrivel

his insides
shriek

I'll take the craft
pick up the tool

find the brother
that needs impact

isn't this how
we evolve

turning corners
giving harbor

yes, I say yes
this is how we evolve

turning corners
and giving harbor

*

your house
makes my senses strong

apparitions
are in the paintings

endless good
inspires your sea

I tremble before
your pull

I'm tempted
to tie things down, though

to prevent any float
or flying off

your smoothness
makes me stop, anxious

I'd rather choke
on fragments

yet, exquisitely
I slip, silent

into the waters
of your love

your grand rolling
peaceful wave

erasing debts
and folly

am I lost
or losing ground

am I who I was
anymore

a voice deep within me
whispers

wait
for what's in store

music in my limbs
seraphim in my psyche

candle, not coin
permeates my soul

opaqueness stirs
dim neutral expands

by sudden vivid glory
I'm engulfed

every fire blazes
hand and hair raises

the trinity's sacrifice
is clear

oh the painful become
of becoming

the tangle of my own
wild wiring

the desire to turn
commence my running

the tocks of clocks
soon expiring

how to fulfill
the best of what's made

draw the bad blood
from the drawing

but draw I must
with shaky trust

unlisten
to death's crow cawing

*

footprints
all over my beloved

her dish
thrown in fury

handprints
on her affection

her fondness now
but fumes

the peace
that was measureless

transformed by chisels
to disarray

tradition
that was weightless

suspects fraud
and personal cut

attractive firsts
all seem over

only withheld grace
is left

nostalgia in a noose
holding its breath

a deadened dusting
impossible to bear

jubilee and yes
a sudden celebration

she'd like to punch scripture
sigh with her wrist

introduce this trellis
to that woman over there

sneak a cushion in
for her seat

tie her hair in knots
have teams remove their armor

tremble before
an erotic scene

fit that fool
into her purse

travel to where
saviors are born

then punch scripture again
take a number, ha

punch and sigh
and take a number

I fuss and fuss
over lessons

but thoughts of travel
intrude

then stones of memory
leave me torn

an uncomfortable vastness
blooms

my soul gets split
for miles and miles

you're here, you're there
you laugh, you cry

maybe I need
to hang past lives

from the squeaky floorboards
above

recline and entertain
effigies of clothes

till merry bells
and safety return

what's the lesson
in your rude lesson

humility spitting
in my face

unravel of fabrics
spinning specters

the collapse of time
and space

well, you are the bloom
the vast, the hanger

the fuss
and unsafe happening

the server of happenstance
and misunderstand

but also the miles
of reclining grace

my memory is not
what I remember of yours

you chose to pick out
and tweak

where I need
chronological fullness

for you, any day
is any day of the week

he tags along
and bellows

has reckless
epic ideas

patches to put on
fences to climb

critics to curse
and damn

once busted
for chaining substances

turning on waterfalls
inside factories

he's grumpy and ready
to label others

posers, wannabes
flowers, fakes

we'll get inside
expose ourselves

piss on this
moon over that

release the chains
drop the cargo

wait for the fire
then run

he spits for pleasure
spits to spit

thinks they're all
with him

but they keep passing
building after building

laughing at his failed
and fallaway railing

*

it's the beginning again
another round in the ring

either I'm a warrior
or an apparition

either I shapeshift
and bloom

put on
my bitter face

or drop through a crack
nobody sees

I practice
in the basement

being framed
point blank

being wild
then an ache

then a place
nobody knows

both the boxer
and the boxed

riled up
empty

yielding bloody scores
at a good clip

maybe I should stay
and say what needs to be said

maybe I should leave
leave the unspoken unspoken

hey, who said anything
about throwing the match

my hand turns out
the bold lamp above me

at school
I'm a cherry that sings

a blob of a body
with ears

a spoon
that thinks it's sharp

a knife that loves
to make collage

I daydream
that I'm a contortionist

slipping
in leafy landslides

that I'm a piece
of difficult art

a sculpture of a twisted
tree limb

that's hollow
and played like a flute

I lose my broken-tooth
comb to the floor

it's kicked out
into the hall

some kind of poverty
unfreshens my face

the actors in me
search their bodies

my illusions swim
in pursuit of me

water fountains
fill up rooms

but I'm above
semiconscious

left for dead
in a tree

my hope is sincere
this holiday

despite the nugget
of perish

I praise the plan
to challenge and cure

while battling
the hinge of doubt

I'm stuck in chains
fully conquered

by the center's
heavy heaving jungle

but I can molt
with pinpointed effort

travel happy
with nomadic tribes

was it I who fainted
or was it the world

when buildings fell
and oceans grew

was it I who slipped
or was it you

when what was said
was too much

remember the hope
my love

remember the hope
forget the rest

someday we'll be stronger
each other's guest

and that feeling
the falling reach

yes, it's good
when it's there

when not
we can always jest

at one time
she threw her beauty at me

*

I don't know
how these valleys broke

or how they can weep
but they do

how these old cold ships
can buzz with truth

how flocks can linger
in a circle

I don't know
your echo's answer

to my initial
stifled question

why your eyes pull
and my eyes don't

why our talk of birds
trails off

why the good Lord made us
blow by blow

to be lean and standing
but barely

I don't know
how these valleys broke

or how they can weep
but they do

how can it be
wisemen don't care

when caring and wisdom
are intertwined

how can it be
that a wise-ass gets it

and
exactly right

she approves of nonsense
today

yearning for fade
picking avenues

being aroused
by hips

retreating
from kaleidoscopic scenes

then dancing back in
backwards

she's a yes for less
an oh-no for more

about-faces then flips
her opinion gladly

a glutton for nothing
then hungry for trees

stuffing in lamb legs
then choosey at a feast

she defines goofy
the very definition of a goof

who oof-trips, golly
over non-ambiguous rugs

we sense the tears
in her fake-faux jewels

but it's perspiration, water
drinks in her face

ice chips
and why she can't see

*

their route
once overlapped waltzes

now their fortune and promise
are preyed upon

a buoyant mix
of gallows and fame

parties of life
unguarded

rich targets dance
before hidden guns

money is stuffed
into mouths

ropes slip down
from the ceiling

knives up like grass
from the floors

the see-through meek
mumble preludes

murmur of possible
tense tomorrows

but joy of joys
these two overlook

overstep, slip around
sign the guest book

declare their holidays
take out the boat

give every reason
for celebrating float

they toast to what was
is now and will be

smash their glasses
for good luck

kiss for the cameras
laugh for no reason

answer breezy questions
in clicks and clucks

dispel the murk
what reporters wrote

then are kicked unconscious
by a gloating goat

the audience thinks
it will be the shovel

or maybe the dagger
in the drawer

but what about the hammer
the handyman wore

or a good old fashioned punch
and kick to the head

maybe the ditch
is deep enough

maybe she'll deny
and claw an escape

catch her skirt
on a ragged corner

leave
a wide swatch of red

it could all move
out to the country

where it's snowing
like a feminine presence

someone could arrive
with prints and steps

someone else
could have taken a trip elsewhere

Tahiti
or Timbuktu

twin brothers
or both ghosts, they wonder

supernatural
or perfectly carnally natural

sex in the pants
and panties of all

masculine plumes
rise in the air

is this the time
to smoke

the goody-goody righteous
peeks up through the floorboards

ready to surprise
the open-shirt maggot

magnify the eye
widen the long

end of the barrel
in the song

he rejected
bounty

drained
all essence

hallucinated
a bad future

watched whirlpools
for weeks, transfixed

waded
into bleak belows

chose to be spun
and lost for years

enlarged the bloody
drawn and quartered

refused to receive
sweet metaphors

vivid reminders
of God

giant cats made of clouds
bears made of stars

planets playing
hula hoop

dogs at the gates
of myth and magic

if only he was
another another

he could settle into
a new foreign land

old lines of sight
to the sidelines

careless and free
with new cares

but he's behind
in every race

and everyone's running
running in place

stamping, stammering
pounding down a story

while zoos and canopies
wild as ever

crowd and yip
for attention

you dream
that you're in prison

that you're in prison
paralyzed

that you're in prison
paralyzed

top
to bottom

bottom
to top

hair
to toenail

blister
to mole

that you're in prison
paralyzed

your fervor frozen
frozen forever

what protected you
stripped away

stripped away
stripped and stripped

the odds in your favor
stripped away

stripped
stripped

and stripped
and stripped

in your favor
and against

tossed
and tossed out

you dream
you're tossed

paralyzed
frozen

your fervor frozen
frozen forever

stripped and stripped
and stripped away

hair to toenail
blister to mole

stripped
and stripped away

tossed
and tossed out

you dream
that you're tossed

paralyzed
lit

others victorious
"victory is ours!"

but you tossed out
paralyzed, blistered

others victorious
"victory is ours!"

but you, hair pulled
and stripped away

fallen
frozen

blistered
paralyzed

others victorious
"victory is ours!"

but you, tossed out
and staked

others victorious
not winners, just victors

and you, staked
and paralyzed

in a dream
a state

in a dream of state
in a stately dream state

you dream
you're in prison

in a state
of battle

with others victorious
"victory is ours!"

and you, paralyzed
with moles and blisters

hair
stripped away

pulled
tossed

staked
by victors

in prison
paralyzed

with bugs
and belongings

the burning
burning

and you, eventually
tossed out

others victorious
"victory is ours!"

the burning
burning

the battle
over

the resistance
fallen

the burning
burning

bugs and belongings
annihilated

only portions of people
and people left

dreams
of glorious design rising

and the burning
burning

sweltering
shuddering

swallowed
by overwhelming darkness

I guess I doubt my list
oh no

my stretch
has become an enemy

goals mourn
over loss of fuel

creatures within
grow chaotic

chemicals want to know
their why

and, dammit
when they will combust

sorcery steals
the second hand

eagles fly off
with my bed

minutes meld
into globs of blub

mellow grey heads
fill my head

and everyone wants
to sleep or get paid

everyone clamors
vacation

I last ditch effort
to plug and not play

but all power gets sucked
into sedation

tired of the pull
of the suffering genius

wouldn't it be swell
to join and swell

daydream of puckers
jot only dots

respond to invitations
to dine

leave the hypnosis
of serpents and scarce

stop the swirl
of oblivion

say goodbye
to blotchy pages

crossed out subpars
and ageless ages

come, let's grab
a random express

to wild and whatever
and whatever happens next

discover funny people
that make announcements

change their minds
and change direction

laugh at the beginnings
of grand voyages

jump in the water
to splash

it's no trouble getting in
and out of trouble

when your dear
is jolly beside you

let's go out
mix up some rabble

and risk
falling on our ash

he speeds to the alley
calculates the hurry

slicks his hair
flips up his collar

where are they, yes
and where is it

wasn't it today
when it was to happen

he checks his watch
his phone, his hearing

pockets, lighter
penpad, eyesight

a bench appears
taunting starts

moments from his past
tower over him

his natural talent
for radical flare

flares up
but isn't enough

it's an act
a painter's brushstroke

not
an authentic smear

he, blank
beefs up his own

but who is he trying
to fool

bravely he sits
in the din of voices

the carousel of sound
the solution

*

where is my melody
tinged and tingling

where are the answers
that once drifted into view

how long ago
did the good drop their weight

when was the last time
the sea called

why would every vibrant hue
mix and mix until grey

why did the hike
drive me to despair

who loosened me up
and distracted me

until everything
came apart

when did my grand plan
of youth collapse

into endless
endless plans

the sea was inspiration
at one time

the good were inspiration
at one time

colors, drift
the weight of things

hikes, drives
the evening out

all
were inspiration

who switched my praise
to hang

yesterday swims
and there's no shore

is heaven endless
treading of water

today's
traces of struggle

gathered contemplation
tender wonder

help me
hope for more

tomorrow, I suspect
will be crazy weather

both brighter and darker
flashy and falling

too hot, too cold
water in every form

I flow through my work
life lifts in my chest

a new child is born
every minute

the same child, though
both me and not me

and you, Lord
not entirely you either

I look for and find
your writing in the sky

star to star
star to star

as if you're connecting
the dots

again and again
I find the same constellations

as if I've forgotten
and must remind myself

to accept what was
is, and will be

my adventure
has crumbled

I've awakened to a meal
without aroma

twilight
is out

beard grown
to the bench

there is no
candied solution

only
too-tight collars

surfaces
of objects

carousels whose tunes
are cranked and tilted

blank
is my reward

I'm a sovereign
fake

what was plum and plural
is now distressed and dead

oh
savor my misery

isn't that what you wanted
all along

for me to grow grey
and squirm

*for my dreams
to take a hike*

*you like to think
you live*

*in a smooth
painting*

*cut bread
with ceremony*

*join your lover
for soup*

*help tie and untie
with ease*

*before you might slip
you stop*

*before any debt
you pay up*

*you like to think
temptation*

has
no pull

but under
your clean white linens

you're
dirty

at the back door
there's no guard

you hope apparitions
will have mercy

that your strong extra-sense
will locate the rot

but you were raised to join
as a sot

*

he's natural, poised
attentive to buffoons

spare in his wit
dependably efficient

puts rooms and yards
back together

of course he'd like
to defile and climax

grab and gospel
and shudder until rusted

undulate against
both aboves and belows

spare no one
his indulgent thrust

but he putters and pays
the right amount

tips generous
listens sympathetic

his brain overheating
his heart racing

sleuth
to backroom slut

he boggles
the grinding mind

being both
humble hut and wanton rut

in check he holds
both check and pelvis

opens doors
for visitors

waits until
he's last to enter

or exit
or enter again

I had the sad chance
to stray from my body

to tame the sharp rain
of the world around me

I could've pushed
to order tongues cut

build into the slender
some muscle

I could've been glad
and feasting at the dance

a man
of mountainous consequence

swaying in my seat
with the windows open

on the ride of the day
each day

instead I'm a character
among other characters

going about variously
and unresolved

you neither gave the chance
nor took it away

it was my choice
and I chose you

*

she whispers something plush
dwells in a riddle

angry
she corners morning

tears always near
plenty to remember

a maze
of gauzy metaphor

weirdly positioned
all knees and elbows

there's dust in the couch
she engages pastels

picks up jewelry
picks up partners

brushes any dirt
away

may I search
your toes

tap open
your fists

act out
the battle

in a grand
manner

breathe
warm hope

to your crestfallen
death

call out
foreign words

to your
ribcage

I believe
your shiver

means life
is at play

your clutch
now belies

considerable
strength

*may I test
the temp*

*of your bath
when you bathe*

*though you're capable
of pinching*

*the round sun
oval*

*out my window
surprise and laughter*

*a dreamy morning
with animals and blankets*

*a fountain spray
creating ghosts*

*that linger
and wander away*

*but I'm inside
midnight walls*

I stand and wait
for the end of evening

conjure the cliffs
I once jumped off

the crazy laughter
I swallowed

the shirts
I tore out of

the pockets
I removed

the glass panes
I broke

so many fingers
without a hand

so many
grasping fingers

*

frankly
I'd like an answer

I'd like
an answer

when letters swirl
I'd like an answer

when the force is despair
I'd like an answer

when the muse is low
and the bottle is drawn

I'd like
an answer

when the fog settles in
and mad brothers spark

and the astral is a mess
and tangos stomp and strangle

them-
selves

that's when I need it most
and always

an
answer

*my questions are good
strong, to the point*

*I send them and they reach
the right megamind*

*the granddaddy of them all
the Being of beings*

*then I wait
pace patient*

*evolve like I should
unscream my scream*

*and feel everything
everything*

*everything
but serenity*

*she battles a drawer
yells into space*

*temperatures go up
fists are made*

an honest tap
breaks

all
privacy

she's grateful for nothing
nothing!

packs up the blossoms
acts out the false

toes are crooked
everything's old

everyone's old
older, shivering

the ribs and cages
are broken and showing

and what about this
the sun goes down

snaps out
as the voyage begins

*some make it to the altar
but don't marry*

*have plenty of sex
but no children*

*some pray like a madman
are never struck by lightning*

*write many words
but say nothing*

*make people laugh
but don't know why*

*run away
when they should've stayed*

*creep up to surprise
when their timing was off*

*make a fortune
but only a little each year*

*

*comments scatter around me
thorns make their way*

the universe weaves tighter
the infinite is left unspoken

such thin pleasures
rewards made of snuff

I arise, leave the party
wade into reverence

deeply weary
I make promises again

my flesh to obey
my internal to remain devout

sad and bold is the eternal
sad and bold am I

I mend the gates
mend the fences

piece the ruins
back together

plant dark grass
pluck what's dry

save each flame
for the fire

I polish the dull
pinch my epiphanies

wait for the bruises
to fade away

choose what's funny
and everything's funny

when random
beats the hell out of control

the water from the faucet
runs splatch to rust

to
clear

I open the windows
for a cross breeze

my thundercloud thoughts
purify, pour

instead of survive
I dive

*

she watches
the wet past

the rosy grapes
and exchanges

acknowledges
the milky nightgowns

the ragged beds
the drunk torches

breasts and clowns
vanish to reappear

journals have pages
torn out and burned

a life she lived
but didn't

a heavy life
for others, about others

a book she read
or really her own

a movie she watched
half-asleep

dramatic episodes
with countless seasons

or a dream
from delirious sickness

get up, move
open something, start

concentrate
on your right hand rising

but the pantry shelf for baking
is empty

the stock
having jumped to the floor

his joke
has a real hallelujah

the miniature question
how to get this top off

becomes a grand
unforgiving road

the land loops
peace fragments

laughter starts
at the knot

ooh ha ha
from bad to worse

the inevitable
crash and clatter

drapes pulled down
along with the bar

a conk on the head
for those that like that

and a soak
that crushes at the end

oh the beauty of it
the continued unrest

everything slippery
to the touch

so much broken glass
the fish flipping

skating
on a piece of ice

halfway up
pulling down another

new splays, new ponds
new spins, new towels

providence has given him
a good righteous poke

once
and for all

I live
in a cellar of willows

proud and comic
both

tearing up
over the slightest thing

the cost of encountering
self

a crazy mix
of attempts to distract

feeling good
about feeling bad

sullen under warbling
warping sheets

of a bed broken down
long gone

welling up
in wells of squalor

my heart burned to ash
in a hearth removed

my north, south
east, west

meager
to a punishing point

absolutely
unfit for fitness

*why get up
and start again*

*with what, as who
do what, by when*

*for who, where to
what now*

*

*his form
bravely veined*

*his poor romance
to be buried*

*soon after innocence
shame*

*soon after reverie
the end*

*still he notes
the sunny mystical*

*listens
to the counsel of the wind*

marvels over the march
and skyward gaze

of flowers
with crowns at their core

near the stream
there's a flutter

a hymn
that's curious

a mass
that's sung by trees

he knows the tune
and hums along

walks
without meaning to walk

a conscience
absentminded

a consciousness lost
and found

you materialize
like a body of haze

your reflection in the sky
as well as the water

I can't reason
you away

I can't drive you away
with questions

I can't risk injury
and rush at you

wave my hand through
to disperse you

when you stay
I can't disappear

when you leave
I can't save you

we're told what is simple
thrives

we're told
to expect zero

greet
every greeting

your stomach
will tell you what to do

but it's a mess
you're a mess, I'm a mess

the webs in the trees
the bracken and weeds

we're all overgrown
spreading, gone to seed

hoping that a timing
will grow some truth

that a coincidence
will draw us back

to
each other

you are the spontaneous
pop-up fair

*a classic
improvisation*

*a vital instrument
performing an instant*

*in an instant
I'm solo and deep*

*I watch the weight
of language*

*feel
the elegant strings*

*slip
on what's illuminated*

*pulse with the tempo
of the forest*

*for me, now
is forever*

*and explosions
are slow*

*

my joy is fragile
stained glass, separated

my fear is fragile
too

clinging to breath
and first words

dear God
throw blankets over the commotion

*

I have the luck
of dust

the drift, the fall
the collecting in the corner

my wisdom
is unconscious

flukes and struggles
run parallel

my life has been
a tapestry

*each day
naively crafted*

*I cross life and wild
and get wildlife*

*animals to tend to
people to feed*

*fences to erect
houses to build*

*but sometimes
my tall sins quiet down*

*and a field of genuine
appears*

*and a prophet calls me
on the phone to say*

*there's a better you
coming, just wait*

*there's a better you coming
just wait*

*

the thing about him is
he's there, you know

he's quiet
but he's loud

but he's quiet, too
and he fidgets

he gets up
decides to sit down

he won't participate
then he blurts

catches himself
looks off in the distance

tries to catch
your eye

so, he's there
he's quiet

and he sits
a lot

I walk
to satisfy

the need
to speak voices

to navigate my secrets
in secret

I bruise my toes
on choose and games

tentacle roots
high-hurdle curbs

then slide into third
the mess of mud

rejoin the army
of the dead

I suspect
this will be a tough verse

no berries or blessings
recovered

only what's next
and next duplicated

the charging
then refusing of grace's entrance

staying within
long parallel lines

no longer able
to see the possible

weighing the totality
of tending just to tend

going through the mammoth
minutiae of motions

what's my name
it doesn't matter anymore

solace, sanctuary
both a farce

kinship with who and what
who cares

the sun may as well
go down in the east

*flipflop
the whole of the source confounds*

*yet you say
your day was strangely rough*

*that you need to talk
and not talk*

*and I listen, waiting
in love with you*

*and this fills what all needs
to be filled*

*the healing is rough
peril gets corrected*

*imbalance bends
to symmetrical stand*

*no trumpets or refuge
for getting up*

*no positive
audience buzz*

just conflict and frustration
less obscure

the ruckus
a bit less of a ruckus

possess me, Lord
take me out of myself

make me
a valuable addition

aren't you the antidote
to being a dolt

can't you take this zealotry
for stuffing stuff

I've been so busy
burying the sand

I've made each grain
more real than real

nothing's growing
oh yes, I've forgotten

seeds are life
itself

*compact, knowing
and only you*

*by your breath
can make them*

*I'm an inward creature
a scrap of solar*

*naive
to the point of a twist*

*I daydream with integrity
labor with courage*

*fill my corner
with energy*

*I watch you twirl
relentless in your blender*

*all colors
becoming one*

*you funnel yourself
to a tall glass*

knock over
and break what you can

what I just read
is distant

sport
feels like a prison

the glow of space and church
has dulled

hope, so familiar
is defiant

how to translate
this narrowing vision

the whole breaking up
moderation dropping out

words escape
like everything else

the room's colors
bleed

*but of all the things
that could come to mind*

*a french lilac
at the bedroom window*

*not now, not recent
but long ago*

*when life was sweet
and new*

*oh the potential
of the next day*

*everything started
growing, changing*

*and nothing
ever finished*

*everything started
worked on, molded*

*clipped and sheared
moved and built up*

stored and abandoned
forgotten, remembered

then
forgotten again

and never
finished

*

no longer ecstatic
for the quest

he returns
to his chunk of challenge

the holiday of luminous
is over

salvation
is paralyzed

intuiting toes
stop wriggling

molted skins
get put back on

arcane heavy histories
weigh landscapes down

even hope wears a coat
that's too big

he tries not to tear
the transparent

handles sincerity
with tender palms

stabs and trashes
strewn ridicule

buries doubt
unboxed

coaxes naive words
from the wind

sets fire
to the peelback of the earth

useless additional parts
of himself

cut out in the bright burning sun
of the day

*

don't underrate
making bad brownies

or asking a stranger
about their dog

smiling at the fritzing
checker in training

praising
their unusual name

it's not as if I've struggled
with a terrible illness

or woke up
suddenly blind or deaf

or unable
to move

it's just
that

*

*I'm learning
to be still*

*to row
without rowing*

*to sing
without singing*

*I have zero polish
at the beach*

*I contact every wave
like a friend*

*play and sweat
in the middle of the pack*

*thank my neighbors
for staying*

*it's okay, I'll be safe
just over this cliff*

I fall, of course
from this hunk

God thumps in me
and I shudder

my drowsy cheek
walks through eden

later, I go to bed
with a sphere

*

a smashed
plum

meditate
on this

*

I can weep no more
dry as bone

I can weep no more
weep no more, weep no more

broken tile
fractured fist

mosaic me
I can weep no more

I can weep no more
fossil of sand

dune of
nothing

wind under the sun
without carry

wind above the sun
without carry

wind stilled beyond
silent vacuum deep

I can weep no more
I can weep no more

*

a child jumps
from a too-high wall

I feel their pain
shoot through my legs

the lip of a woman
shot through the chest

I snarl, slugged back
by the sudden impact

an elderly man
blank with dementia

robs me
of all color and movement

an anxious teen
looking to alight

sends me
into spacious aflutter

*

a suffering mouth
made of dark matter

snarls something
backwards

*

she hungers
for conversation

on this day
of grey elbows

puts on a robe
decked in petals

she yearns for meaning
from rust and blades

to connect with the skin
of her hands

blankets off-kilter
knees around pillows

she attempts to stop the judge
that drums in her head

goes on the fly
to the nearby harbor

to watch the slow boats
and the birds above

*what is there to fasten
unfasten, fix*

*what is odd that should be
made even*

*she alternates
being overwhelmed and blank*

*but the questions
continue to crowd*

*if only the forgotten
splendor of her yard*

*forgot, once and for all
about her*

*when it came
over me*

*my mind tuned
to the tuning fork*

*my heart fell apart
my face broke*

my eyes
stopped moving

when it came
over me

my breath got caught
in the spokes of a wheel

my fingers stopped fiddling
a rhythm

every inch relaxed
and fell to the floor

sweat broke out
where I don't sweat

when it came
over me

a flood
of light and water and blood

flowed through the windows
and out the doors

my insides decided
they didn't want

to be inside
anymore

the warm breeze
shifted cold

a shiver
turned to trembling

the floor became
an icy surface

a frozen
lake

wrap me till I'm hot
and can't move

stop the horns and antlers
from jousting

the table from flying
across the room

settle down
scream

be quiet
fists

lay low
tears

fuss
no more

hold me back
I said hold me back

are you holding me
stronger

use some muscle
I'm gonna

why I'm gonna
just you wait

I'm gonna
now hold me back

*you better hold me back
cause I'm about to*

*there's no telling what
I'm going blind I'm so*

*

*do you have a match?
a flashlight?*

*

*there is no comfort
in the clearing*

*spikes of grass
wallops of weeds*

*

*I contemplate
a sinking in my throat*

*you contemplate
a lake surrounded by forest*

I contemplate
a grave that's a box

you contemplate
ethereal stillness

I send attempts
little tries, little hurts

you send humor
a lively sculpture

what is it with you
must you wink

did you notice me
off-balance, keeling

must it always be
symmetrical

is your world
so even-steven

I turn the tables
you right them

I rage at the stars
you gobble them up

I stare you down
you go about your business

happy to watch
the sunset

happy to watch
the sunrise

either way it's the sun
you say, and colorful

*

a sunflower
closing up

for
the night

a bee
flinching

on
the sidewalk

meditate
meditate

try to meditate
on this

*

it's hard to remember
the wonder of clouds

the crazy joy
of running

the longing
for a kiss

but
I'm still alive

*

is this on
am I on right now

do you care
I'm kidding

not really
anyway, is this on

*

a finger pointing
with no hand

an eye drifting
with no body

a thought
dismantled

a song
without notes

the connective nothing
that connects other nothings

meditate
on this

and that
and this

the resounding silence
of blam

the lean toward
and pull away

the pull apart
and gather

the breathing in
by air itself

the space
beyond the space we know

a grave
turned inside out

meditate
on this

and
more

a waterfall
falling up

the curve
of straight lines

the heart
beating faster

slower
then not

the love
that looks

but doesn't
see

the care
that brushes you away

long
before you ask

the interstellar
without gravity

doors
that open themselves

dirt that dreams
of mountains

mountains that faint
before skies

marbles deciding
to chip themselves

birds landing
on a platter

*a mile-high
rose*

*dropping
petals*

*meditate
on this*

*I leave you
to you*

*roam blank
in the wilderness*

*shake down trees
lose weight*

*break my back
live off bones*

*no flocks in the blue
to follow*

no tomorrows
to gather and clean

only distant fires
falling

only the lonely
crying near the dead

*

I explode inward
over time

I explode outward
over time

what mood
strikes the match

what force
snuffs the flame

*

I
am a child of ink

my pen moves fresh
into weeds

aqua ponds
open up

to swans
made of lemons

maroon footprints
walk room to room

deserted stories
reach out to me

I play between
the spin of spheres

pulses heavy
low, precise

the rumblings make
their mark on me

I belong
to the cycle of volumes

on the smaller scale
change drops from pockets

I step in scrupulous
with care

pick up heads
and far-out tales

stuff them in baskets
boxes, drawers

a spillover brain
with deepening grooves

an ever-new take
on tangle

one friend writes
nimble scripts

another
hands out bibles

yet another rigs
roiling rhythms

backdrops
for speeches

a chamber music
is horribly made

politicians
seek and greet

mobs of maleficent horns
gather

hoot and hound
through the sound

claims of clairvoyance
their high being higher

they aspire to dig in and fight
or die

learning so much
in the muck's mire

sonatinas are for pussies
that fly

offering up cheers
and triggers pulled

bullets shower
an aurora borealis

intense group grind
and explosive release

fixated on callous
and phallus

who do they serve
heaven or fire

is it damn or dam
that bursts

with a crazy roar
it's string up the liar

we're ready for a history
of firsts

always ambitious
all over the place

drunk on adrenaline
and options

each hour
a new hot life to be lived

her goals are here
and everywhere

young, invincible
just getting started

every oyster
her oyster

a mile-a-minute
mountain of mind

a laundry list
of do can-do

run a cafe
be a birthday clown

bolt on spares
and handles

decorate beds
in hotel rooms

rescue
blind dogs

compute
the velvet velocity

of competing trains
on tracks

stack floors
and ceilings

for
geometric skyscrapers

stroll the bays
for garbage

vanish
for the magician

pick peaches
pit peaches

light
the Olympic torch

drink the drunks
under the table

print
gritty erotica

attend
to the dying faithless

juxtapose
bad art

so many lives
waiting to be lived

she buys
the multiverse idea

that she'll come back
again and again

to suck and spit
every flavor

*

this was not
to be the narrative

chaotic snaps
and crying

then soothing gentle
hair and shoulder

oh dreary twists
of fate

secrets planted
mingled with swerve

playing at follow
the leader

seraphim silently knowing
better

circling
the almost dead

who's the transparent
flower now

maybe neither
and never was

how swoon can trick
make trials

but also plant roots
around roots

to my beat-up blur
be kind

to my simple, tall
unconscious clouds

of yearning search
be kind

killer illusions
of unfunny folly

help me guide
and disguise

build up terrains
of mountains and rains

decorate final
chastisements

I so want to be
a something else

a someone whose else
is certain and good

who fits the peel
and motion of together

communes with ease
and pleases

lop off my loopy
give away my before

toss this weathered
wounded heart

oh to be still
and right in the world

oh to be grand
in you

I rehearse
my curiosity

dwell
in a depth of vines

go to where life
starves itself

then stop
the greedy on the street

hitchhike
to the land of drowsy

where breezes
lullaby the sleepy

boomerang
to the city of frantic

where inanimate objects
are on the run

where everyday
conversation is shouted

and guns
barely stun

safe nowhere
curled eyelashes and hair

placated by a plate
of pastries

we step into a stream
of constant steam

disappear
in a hundred years

I'm startled by the laugh
of an opening curtain

the joker
hasn't even started joking

the choking
hasn't even started choking

still
I'm startled by the laugh

*

I have something mad
in my pocket

a smarting hum
under my shirt

a snippy door
that grant's no one

an easy-breezy
entrance

try and shatter my knees
go ahead

blow out my mind
roam with sword

*I've been through this
over and again*

*the reassembly
of whatever and when*

*the wait for whenever
to finally become then*

*hungry
beyond the path*

*beyond
daily bread*

*far beyond
trim and cloth*

*I range
unsubtle*

*harass
every billow*

*marvel over
backsides*

whip up
monkeys

my make
is on the make

a rake
raking

I ride in my own
grand processional

imagine grabbing
clips and clops

pay for nothing
delight in echoes

pause only
to pour and pour

this flowing dream
of curvy sprite

drags earth down
to carnal heaven

topsy turvy
no peace in pieces

clinging to satisfy
the unsatisfied

*

my comedy
is my tragedy

my tragedy
a gag

I developed
goofy expressions

from the deep-deep
ask

turned
my troubled knowing

into egoless
explosions

vibrating anger
became radiant glow

weighty plethora
became plentiful smile

I massaged the burning
purification process

to hot-crossed
buns

resolved the fall
of crushing boulders

and put pebbles
on display

my legacy
is nondramatic

treasureless
till a joke

I've sanctified
compare, contrast

by scrambling in
a yoke

asymmetrical
to a fault

off-balance
and a klutz

*I tried to try
to halt gestalt*

*to be two bitz
more than a futz*

*but here I am
a clam unclammed*

*buffeted
by kingly wave*

*finally washed
to your shimmering shore*

*of hollowed out
and hungry cave*

*he yearns
to fade in prison*

*to climax
in a church*

*to scoot along
in molten lava*

to shiver
without pajamas

to retreat
into a kaleidoscope

put a quick lid
on birdsong

narrow all glow
to a point and out

face the gospels
defiant

make the cosmic
faint from hunger

pick away at peace
till it fights

touch up familiar faces
till ambiguous

make dull
the exciting life

destroy, scratch out
erase, deny

scribble over, break apart
burn, bury

drown, choke
scalp, deface

translate
to another medium

*

he was born
to steward

shapes
toward words

shadows
toward talent

clues
toward solution

fences are there for a reason
he'd say

some days
leave us heaving

mercy isn't
a stage show

it's good to anoint
the elemental

pointless to rebel
against the spectral

gifts are to be opened
in thanks

salvation is sometimes
in freeze or swelter

treasure is formed
when you touch

share your whole share
without reservation

empty may feel rested
in the morning

remember
the choreographed shepherds

the star
is wherever you are

*

hard white stomach
family of oceans

body in rage
about food and love

lightning combs
the hairs of this prince

he's the true catch
of the festival

he'll take any keys
call for what he wants

send ghosts away
like receding fog

he owns the land
and the scattered seed

what grows, what doesn't
who runs, who's caught

empty the nets
what's the best of the treasure

*he's hungry, he's ready
to root and rout*

*descend on death
the ultimate slate*

*encroach
on the final roach*

*oh how he hogs
and thorny horns*

*works hard to muss
the ineffable*

*but the dirty swings exude
eking out*

*and this means nothing
to eternity*

*surprise
a trail of frogs calling*

*surprise
a bridge of marrow*

a waterfall
a rush of words

a raft
leading to doors

surprise
a tribe remembers you

your healthy
innermost

your plans that greet
and benefit

the rouge of you
bleeding out

your unlived ache
begins in the middle

a riot of animals
transforms

you're there but also
used up

skin around the feet
of the new

*

*I hide in the water
in the blur, in the paint*

*chime mysterious
in frightened eyes*

*reveal
genuine emergency*

*breathe up and out
caught cries*

*I try to revive
first features of strong*

*manifest
a tabernacle favor*

*a will beyond my own
the courage to groan*

*break open, let out
the imp of impossible*

*evil creature, sinful swine
wicked winks covered in brine*

hackles and cackles
crash through the wall

are driven from me
the length of the tall

in shock, without blink
I allow the sink

to richly deserved
catatonia

finally safe
from the hoods and the hiss

the rounded fall
to coma bliss

fully awake
but fully asleep

having heeded and returned
heaven's kiss

*

I and my limbs
bark at the grave

slap jovial
any push

applaud the manicured
perfect lawn

hush my mouth
till it's closed

wrong to be pliant
I march away certain

through meadows
not meant to be mine

reach a reflection
who is this person

that grabs and fusses
in the air

closing out
regardless of choice

linens fall gently
on my face

the final tug is tender
subtle

*what's over is done
now grace*

*I'll wait
at the holiday gathering*

*at the silent cemetery
too*

*shelter with my elbows
like an idiot*

*wait for last drops
of you*

*try and knit answers
of diverse escape*

*hasten to every creak
and bell*

*floors and doors
all entry ways*

*for you to arrive
or hell*

I'll climb unhurried
the soft hill

where first you displayed
your array

told of grave powers
that pull at you

laughed
as you toyed with my day

here, play with me
I won't object

I'd like to be fastened
to your gown

be pulled through the sloppy
muddy meadows

of upside down
my smile a frown

for the light's gone out
I'm blinded by dull

if I call out
will you answer

appear calmly
from around a tree

having stolen the dance
from the dancer

can you re-reconvene
with me

fasten the stars
back into the sky

fasten the stars
in the water before us

as well as the stars
in my eyes

I'll wait
at the holiday gathering

at the silent cemetery
too

shelter with my elbows
like an idiot

wait for last drops
of you

*

his emotions grow
like unlocked zoos

no rules, no logic
no command center

storm clouds break
to visions of particles

bits of bad story
everywhere

seeds in flight
clever slight

faith in the wages
of not fine

he practices rage
on a growing stage

then fakes reining in
the rain

he blows
and blows it

links it all
together

one grand theory
of suspicious string

black holes and white holes
ad infinitum

sucking and spewing
the universe

victory is everyone else's
see

I was dealt
the bummest hand

where do you go
when your two legs are tied

and it's hard enough
to just stand

I struggle
with struggle

turn wildlife
to wildfire

why do I make luck
hard

I weave in and out
when standing is sufficient

when stillness
would bring me joy

I kick up dust
create a storm

of particles
I can't see through

the particles themselves
would just as soon

float down
be counted, absorbed

I turn pleasant valleys
into hills to climb

make parallel lines
cross

I trip myself
fall into sin

knowing full well
I pursued it

I know I'm naive
suspect I'm dumb

I'm only enlightened
as a fluke

I may appear
a quiet field

but I scatter
what falls from the cupboard

happy to build
happy to nest

but good
at making things worse

you could introduce me
to my very own prophet

I'd find a way
to squash the future

you could make for me
the perfect potion

to thin all my fat things
out

I would naturally, instinctually
spill the sacred nectar

turn the wrong way
eat the wrong thing

give what I don't have
heap on useless chores

miss the dead end
say something off-color

forget the birthday
complicate the simple

laugh
when I should be silent

so what do you do
when easy isn't easy

and comfortable
freaks you out

when yelling "relax"
winds you up

when your mind
needs constant attention

wings come to warn me
of decay

that so what
is attached to where

that how
may be in the wine and whine

that weapons
may be in my stare

do not partake
in part of it

decide not one
but none

discount the head
that counts and counts

foster long chapters
of rare

detach from the race
the flip-around face

take your seat
a new pupil of air

let the flutter and fold
of thousands of wings

prepare you
for love's dare

porous afternoon
of messiahs

tormented
intelligence

impossible worlds
descend

collisions
loosen

*planes permeate
all views*

*commune with me
with everything*

*redeem yourself
by the fire*

*sing of the sodden
sanctified*

*your liar
now a lyre*

*seeing pain
has to be okay*

*a criss-crossed brain
has to be okay*

*seizures, x-rays
forgetting the year*

*piercing light
clogged veins*

cold blocks
geyser hearts

eyes that dry
in their sockets

unborn babies
in pockets

there's glory
in awareness

even in shock
even in desperate trenches

*

I hold you
when unrequited love

becomes a bitter spit
of sonnet

when distrust blossoms
bilious black

when sugar
no longer is sweet

*

you could've been pure
without blemish

kind
from beginning to end

but you weren't
you were human

slapped others
blithely broke hearts

stepped on toes
ground your heels in

riddled us with gunshots
looked the other way

when the blood
was too much

you could've professed
your love

from the mountaintops
from the top of the ladder at least

*or when looking up
from the basement stairs*

*when the only shine
was the shimmer of ghosts*

*in
the dark*

*but you didn't
you were human*

*you withheld
hemmed and hawed*

*took your time
dragged your heels*

*filed your nails
picked your teeth*

*flossed and brushed
spat and swallowed*

*swished
and spat again*

drowning
I drag you

to the summer's
shore

dry you off
feed you

check
your broken jaw

*

I pine
in the silence

crush
reach out

hidden
forbidden

reach
without reaching

yearn
without anyone knowing

out of step and old
old-fashioned

who pines and yearns
anymore

bleeds profusely
into their hands

chooses to die
a thousand deaths

and you, so beautiful
you, so handsome

synced and new
ageless, certain

alive every moment
the edge of fire

the reason for dance
to begin

that spark, your spark
pulse, zimminess

electricity
that crackles and beams

you're fun and funny
open, tender

eyes so lighthearted
and quick

in a glance, there's music
past the music, more music

past that, even more
your music, ours

the music of the spheres
of creation itself

infinitely deep
and wide

does there have
to be a reason

a hand-in-hand
an in-step, in-line

a heart-to-heart
that's synchronized

haven't there been
reasonless outgrowths

happenings
that are happenstance

random stubs
wicked falls

about faces
prickles, tingles

slaps, punches
indigestion

nerves, grades
slipping off chairs

evals with malice
letters from strangers

bird poop, slug squirt
surprise mirrors

hollows hollowed out
missing eyes

when my mouth is ready
with its gibberish

to fend off other views
and the demons of the world

there's a tone that starts
a sense that develops

in the distance
but coming ever closer

a tone on a vowel
a sense of oo and wonder

an oo that never breathes
that never grows to oh

a forever single oo
that's you

what was I thinking
when I started the car

revved the engine
kept it from dying

when I stopped typing
and stared at my hands

floating above
the keyboard

what started
the waterworks

what was I searching for
when shifting my eyes

when I whisked
all hanging clothes to the side

when I boxed up shoes
tossed cereal in the cart

what is wrong
with me

vegetables aren't
inherently sad

the checker's name, Sam
isn't tragic

booting the computer
isn't a death knell

walking the neighborhood
isn't going in circles

not everything is
a symbol worth mining

a pain worth exploring
a hurt of significance

but here I am
newly strangled

trying to choose
what movie to watch

turning away
from the party conversation

looking for a doorway
out

what about the music
made my heart soar

then sore
the other sore

were the violins
so beautiful

I couldn't help
but weep

had the flock
found new ways to waft

was the air so cold
and dry and bold

I couldn't help
but tearing up

I thought
I'd rock myself

cry tender
grateful tears

into
eternity

then
my hair caught fire

*

it's the stab of light
when your eyes cross the sun

it's the reason
the canker sore started

it's when you clutch
your heart for love

when the darkness that comes
from the edges

over-
whelms

when I turn
to the right

the stuff to the left
slips off the face of the world

when I turn
to the left

the left is back
and jolly

happy to be playing
its tricks

*

when I look up
the floor drops below me

the earth speeds
to the abyss

when I look down
the earth bounces back

trembling
invigorated

*

yesterday is death
let it dictate nothing

stay rugged and vocal
in this holy mess of moments

this, here
is your loudsilent spark

your hallelujah glare
your stand alone time

in the exploding
sun

from richly gifting
flowing ebbs

drink
and drink again

and when you can't
drink anymore

splash
your newfound face

ask for help
enlist other drinkers

splash them, too
take a swimming bath

and when you know
to collect yourself

to move a little less raucous
or rowdy

pour your arms
into evening

flow lightwaterlove
with a rush to others

who need their own core
quickening

he's in love with you
he can smell you

he knows what you look like
under your clothes

he's seen you at your worst
brooding and hateful

throwing rocks through windows
narrowing your eyes

he's heard the words
you yell at bad drivers

232

watched you smack
your shins with your racket

he's touched your bruises
blown away dirt

cleaned the bleeding slits
you made on your arm

he's breathed in unison
when you've stared at the ceiling

got up with you
when you've been restless

watched you pick up
shards of glass

drop tools
on people's toes

he's sat with you
when snacking at 3

kissed you
when you've finally fallen asleep

roused you
when you couldn't stop

bad dreams
from murdering your children

he's heard you call the dead
ingrates

watched you gather friends
to pull them apart

waited nearby
while you argued with family

when you flew into rages
shut doors on fingers

he's seen you
not go to the hospital

to visit
the suddenly dying

he's tasted your mockery
of weirdos and weaklings

watched you preen
before mirrors

when you point out
the goofs of the goofy

he's there when you
trip up the innocent

and trip
the gangly

when you steal
a piece of peppermint candy

forget to pay
for coffee

he's there when you exaggerate pay
on your resume

have sex with your friend
on break at work

masturbate
and wipe your hands on socks

he waits
until you're done

he waits while you wash your hands
and dry them

he walks with you
when you walk away

he stood beside you
when you were ready to jump

to pull the trigger
drop the appliance in

he's watched you punch walls
smile without smiling

shock your body
deplete your reserves

rage and weep
and rage again

till you slumped into years
of the living dead

he's waited for the rage
and sadness to pass

the heaving waves
of drug-crazy moods

he's felt your emptiness
and understood

smelled your fear
redirected the hose

he's breathed on you
when you were choking, seizing up

he's shared his air
when you could hardly move

he's heard you reveal
others' secrets

he's seen you peel out
and swerve

he's heard you sobbing
your eyes squeezed

going over
that terrible decision again

angry with yourself
for a life half-lived

sad that time
is running out

he's witnessed you fussing
and gussying up

making a mess
for fanciness

then drunk and hungry
at party central

out
of control

digging for dirt
kicking up your heels

throwing up in the toilet
passing out under the sink

he closes the door
pulls the drapes

flushes it down
wakes you up

averts your eyes
puts a new towel in the cabinet

for you
to find

he stood by
while you chose

your sharpest words
for maximum laceration

when you recoiled
from a brave healing touch

when you went home
with a strange stranger

he was the silent wave of music
the times you rocked yourself

when nothing mattered
yet everything did

when your heart was broken
for good

he closed your eyes
when you couldn't look anymore

changed the channel
when you were daydreaming

encouraged the dogs
to join you on the bed

sent out a stray cat
on your walk

he loosened your heart
when it beat wildly

allowed gravity
to loosen its grip

stirred up sweet stirrings
of love and desire

after you were sure
you were dead

he lays out fresh clothes
brightens the day

gives the heavy rain
a beautiful sound

drives you home
walks you in

pulls the covers
up to your chin

and you wake up
somewhere, down the line

as if
in a fresh new dream

he puts you on the road
to a beautiful nowhere

the long
muddy shovel

work that's gloriously dirty
and hard

the more
that's never over

start a track
of roughhewn bed

go down the raw road
and see

how plans and plantings
withhold their bloom

while sidelong glances
fruit

oh the sex
that grows each drop

makes each shape
bulge and shiver

the expansion of animals
the universe's jungle

within each cherish
neverending

*

he's awake
before you are

watches
you come to

knows
you look past him

that you don't want
to be seen

*

he's
at your work

shares
a cubicle

sits
at your dining room table

*he's
in the shower stall*

*when you go
to the bathroom*

*standing
on the dance floor*

*when you do your move
maniacal*

*in
the passenger seat*

*when you're hitting
the steering wheel*

*he's seen you wait
to make that call*

*for days
for weeks*

*until the person
was dead*

*

he knows
you feel fat

that you call others
fat

he's seen you
insert yourself

between lovers
and friends

heard you
make up stories

to make others
squirm

frequently you want
a quick fix

of laughter
and squeals

come on
jeez

what fun is that
you think you're fun

you enjoy a good funnin'
you're flippin' funnin' now

huh
start again, chump change

*

I'm afraid the approaching mob
will riot

but it doesn't take
a riotous mob

thundering toward
or through

I'm afraid
of a single angel

afraid of random noises
and nonsense

afraid
of quiet reason, too

*it could be
anything*

*really
anything*

*and any moment
now*

*here is what I remember
from the party:*

*hi, I'm so-and-so
nice to want you*

*are you funny?
no*

*a standup?
no*

*you should be
no*

*excuse me
dude*

bro
bru

I don't like to talk
I do

I'm an observer
an observer

I'm auditing
back of the class

what's in the punch?
what's that note?

I make up little songs
three seconds long

I exist
therefore I feel

sexual energy
humping the fridge

going down
on the pile of coats

satyrs in their drinks
synchronous eye shifts

my girlfriend
that's her over there

uh huh
taking a bite of that plant

bursts of mouths
caught laughter

wide-eyed wonder
under butterfly glasses

paintings
shuffling themselves on the walls

the playing cards
locked in a box

sexual energy
in the walls

eyes in the sockets
of the chandelier

anyone bring a mic?
Mike, of course

an amp?
Mike

stage?
Mike

is so-and-so here?
I love so-and-so

Mr. Pulitzer-Fulbright?
not really, no

is Will here?
you can't will a poem

Will can
he thinks he can

D.O.A.
. . .

"Earth in my mouth
Mars in my eyes

Jupiter belly
Saturn wrists"

verses again
everything's versus

isms, yuck
let's talk prose

let's just
talk

no
sing

no
pray

anything else
have sex, yes

she's a toothpick, yes
let's write about a toothpick

she's an estuary, yes
let's write about that

she's a voluptuary, well
it'll take some doing

but yes
let's write about that

so where
do you work?

a cave
the zoo

*the movie house
womb*

*vagina
theater*

*I'm playful and morose
a sweet puppy, dead*

*on the welcome mat
no less*

*I don't understand you
nor me myself*

*philosophy for me
go ahead, all ears*

*let's restore the silence
turn off the mic*

*I'm best
yes?*

*when I
disintegrate*

*

David Paul Mesler is a classically trained jazz musician and educator known for his 45 albums on ECR, his 15 major Hollywood films, his performances for 1000s of events including for 4 sitting US Presidents, leading the jazz band at Benaroya Hall for 10 years, his 100s of original art songs and chamber works, and his 28 years of teaching music at Seattle Central and North Seattle Colleges. As a pianist, David's film credits include The Blind Side (2009), Warm Bodies (2013), The Sisterhood of the Traveling Pants (2005), Battlefield Earth (2000), and The Wrong Guy (1997), as well as the Emmy Award winning television features for Disney, Eloise at the Plaza (2003), and Eloise at Christmastime (2003). David himself was nominated for a Northwest Regional Emmy in 1992. He is a prolific maker of experimental films and digital art, and has been writing poetry since age 16.

davidpaulmesler.com

DAVID'S THANKS GO OUT TO

Family and friends for their understanding, love and support; teachers and mentors for their inspiring influences; favorite composers, musicians, poets, and filmmakers for their endlessly intriguing body of work; and students and colleagues at Seattle Central and North Seattle Colleges.

DAVID'S SPECIAL THANKS GO OUT TO

Jocelyn, Nathan, Nicholas, John Sundsten, Jim Hopkins, Kenneth Ernst, Barbara Moneymaker, Morton Lauridsen, Elmer Bernstein, Christopher Young, Buddy Baker, Jerry Goldsmith, Milt Larsen, Richard Sherman, Robert Sherman, Jan MacDonald, Troy Skubitz, Annemarie Guzy, Larry Feder, Linda Bonomi, Kit Herrod, Shelley Kuni, Jared Erlandson, Monique Johnson, Jan Oppelaar, Rosetta Hunter, Jim Cauter, Anthony Spain, Karen Rice, Julie Reed, George Shangrow, Scott Spain, David Harrington, David Sabee, Simon James, Alan and Hinako Hovhaness, Tony Rondolone, Tom Dziekonski, Ellen Finn, Mike Dennis, Michael Nicolella, Katherine Moore, Barbara Hume, Kelly Hume, Pip McCaslin, Julia, Dan, Gary, and Scott, SMPTV friends at USC, Mike Hickey, Sebastian Denault, Bonnie Murphy, Jeffrey Pettijohn, Mikiech

Nichols, Matthew Merlino, Hezza Fezza, Louise Matoso, KT Niehoff, Greg Bartholomew, Dee Dee Evergreen, Jennifer Oliver, Doug Palmer, Jane Cater, Rebekah Naumann, Jon Shirley, Sheryl Neupert, Doug Haire, Steve Vitore, Adam Burd, Johnny Mendoza, Stuart Hallerman, Fika, and Josh Hansen.

. . .

Made in the USA
Middletown, DE
27 October 2025

20130191R10146